My Favorite Dogs

POODLE

Jinny Johnson

A+

Smart Apple Media

Published by Smart Apple Media
P.O. Box 1329
Mankato, MN 56002

Printed in the United States of America,
at Corporate Graphics in North Mankato, Minnesota.

Designed by Hel James
Edited by Mary-Jane Wilkins

Library of Congress Cataloging-in-Publication Data

Johnson, Jinny, 1949-
    Poodle / by Jinny Johnson.
       p. cm. -- (My favorite dog)
    Includes index.
    Summary: "Describes the care, training, and rearing of the poodle. Also explains
the poodle's unique characteristics and history"--Provided by publisher.
    ISBN 978-1-59920-845-9 (hardcover, library bound)
    1. Poodles--Juvenile literature. I. Title.
    SF429.P85J64 2013
    636.72'8--dc23
                          2012012146

Photo acknowledgements
t = top, b = bottom, l = left, r = right
page 1 iStockphoto/Thinkstock; 3 Jagodka/Shutterstock; 4-5 Utekhina Anna/
Shutterstock; 6-7 Hemera/Thinkstock; 8-9 Hemera/Thinkstock; 10 iStockphoto/
Thinkstock; 11 Dale C. Spartas/Corbis; 12t Jagodka/Shutterstock, b Hemera/
Thinkstock; VitCOM Photo/Shutterstock; 14 iStockphoto/Thinkstock; 15l Eric
Isselée/Shutterstock; r iStockphoto/Thinkstock; 16 iStockphoto/Thinkstock;
17 iStockphoto/Thinkstock; 18 Getty Images; 19 Paul A. Souders/Corbis;
20 Eric Isselée/Shutterstock; 22 sonya etchison/Shutterstock; 22 George
Doyle,Stockbyte; 23 Hemera/Thinkstock
Cover iStockphoto/Thinkstock

DAD0504a
112012
9 8 7 6 5 4 3 2

Contents

I'm a Poodle!

People say I'm handsome and I'm also smart, friendly, and easy to live with.

I'm gentle, playful, and good company. I'm a great family dog.

5

What I Need

I'm active and a fast runner. I like to have plenty of exercise every day.

I love being with people, and I like to make my family smile.

I'm not happy if I'm left
on my own for
a long time.

The Poodle

Straight tail, held upright (often docked or shortened)

Color: solid colors, including gray, white, apricot, brown, and black

Height: three sizes. Standard: over 15 inches (38 cm) at shoulders Miniature: 10–15 inches (25½–38 cm) Toy: up to 10 inches (25½ cm)

Thick curly coat, may be clipped

Small feet

Alert expression

Long ears hang close to head

Dark, oval-shaped eyes

Long, slender muzzle

Black nose

Sturdy chest

Proud, upright posture

9

All About Poodles

Poodles were first bred as working dogs. Hunters used them to fetch game birds from water.

When the dogs went into the water their thick coats got soaked and it was hard for them to swim. The owners trimmed the hair so the dogs could move more easily. They left thick hair in places that needed to be kept warm, such as the ankles and chest. So that's the reason for the poodle's trim.

Growing Up

Poodle pups need to stay with their mom until they are about eight weeks old.

When you first take your puppy home he may be frightened at first and miss his family. Be very kind and gentle while he gets used to you.

Show Dogs

Most owners like their dog's coat to be short and neat. Keep the hair on the face and feet clipped to help the dog stay clean.

If you want to enter your poodle in dog shows, he will

need a poodle clip. Parts of his body and tail will be shaved, as well as his face. He should

have pom-poms on his ankles and tail. There are several different styles of clip.

Training Your Dog

Poodles are one of the most intelligent breeds of dog. They learn quickly and like to please, so they are easy to train.

Poodles perform well at agility trials.

These dogs like to entertain their owners and can be taught tricks. Poodles used to work as circus dogs and were popular performers.

Working Dogs

A poodle's brains and good temper make it a good working dog. Poodles work as search and rescue dogs, and can be trained to sniff out forbidden items

A poodle service dog waits near his owner.

at airports. They make great
seeing-eye dogs for blind people.

Poodles also race against huskies
in sled races in Alaska and Canada.

Your Healthy Poodle

A poodle's hair will grow and grow. It needs regular trimming, even if you don't want to clip your dog's coat into fancy patterns.

Your dog's coat will need regular
brushing and combing. Some owners
gather the hair on the top of the
dog's head into a topknot.

Poodles can have eye problems,
so take your dog to the vet if you
notice any signs of these.

Caring For Your Poodle

You and your family must think very carefully before buying a poodle. Remember, he may live as long as 14 years.

Every day your dog must have food, water, and exercise, as

well as lots of love and care. He will
also need to be taken to the vet for
regular checks and vaccinations.

When you and your family go out
or away on vacation, you will have
to make plans for your dog to be
looked after.

Useful Words

agility trials
Events where dogs run around courses with obstacles and jumps.

huskies
Type of dogs used to pull sleds.

vaccinations
Injections given by the vet to protect your dog against certain illnesses.

Index